W9-BNP-608

Nature's Wonders

THE GRAND CANYON

BYRON AUGUSTIN
AND JAKE KUBENA

 **Marshall Cavendish**
Benchmark
New York

Marshall Cavendish Benchmark
99 White Plains Road
Tarrytown, NY 10591
www.marshallcavendish.us

Expert Reader: MaryLynn Quartaroli, Nexus Math/Science
NAU Project Director, Northern Arizona University, Flagstaff

All Internet addresses were correct and accurate at the time of printing.

Library of Congress Cataloging-in-Publication Data
Augustin, Byron.
The Grand Canyon / by Byron Augustin and Jake Kubena.
p. cm. — (Nature's wonders)
Summary: "Provides comprehensive information on the geography, history, wildlife, peoples,
and environmental issues of the Grand Canyon"—Provided by publisher.
Includes bibliographical references and index.
ISBN 978-0-7614-3935-6
1. Grand Canyon (Ariz.)—Juvenile literature. 2. Grand Canyon (Ariz.)—Geography—Juvenile literature. 3. Grand
Canyon (Ariz.)—History—Juvenile literature. 4. Natural history—Arizona—Grand Canyon—Juvenile literature.
5. Grand Canyon (Ariz.)—Environmental conditions—Juvenile literature. I. Kubena, Jake, 1982– II. Title.
F788.A 89 2010
979.1'32—dc22
2008041231

Editor: Christine Florie
Publisher: Michelle Bisson
Art Director: Anahid Hamparian
Series Designer: Kay Petronio

Photo research by Connie Gardner

Cover photo by Antar Dayal/Illustrative Works/Corbis

The photographs in this book are used by permission and through the courtesy of: *Corbis:* Pat O'Hara, 4; David
Muench, 17; Tom Bean, 22, 60; George H. H. Huey, 28; Stefano Amantini, 39; Bettmann, 42; Antar Dayal/
Illustrative Works, 44; Galen Rowell, 68; *NorthWind Picture Archive:* 50, 51; *Tom Bean:* 9, 10–11, 15, 20, 59, 72;
Minden Pictures: Yva Momatiuk and John Eastcott, 12; Carr Clifton, 35; Cyril Ruoso, 38; Scott Leslie, 81; ZSSD,
82; *Animals, Animals:* Ruth Cole, 33(T), Zigmund, 33(B); *SuperStock:* age footstock, 25, 61; Tom Algire, 86–87; *AP
Photo:* Ross Franklin, 64–65, 66; *Getty Images:* Carr Clifton, 27; Jeff Foott, 31, 89(T); Joe McDonald, 32; David
Hiser, 54; Rainer Grosskopf, 71; Walter Meayers Edwards, 79; Time/Life, 89(B); *The Image Works:* Mary Evans
Picture Library, 40; *Art Life:* Travelstock collection, 30; *Alamy:* Zach Holmes, 75, William Leaman, 84.

Maps (p. 6 and p. 16) by Mapping Specialists Limited

Printed in Malaysia

1 3 5 6 4 2

CONTENTS

ONE

A Slice through Time

The Grand Canyon is one of the best-known landforms in the world. Created primarily by the erosional power of the Colorado River, it reaches across much of northern Arizona. The canyon is located in one of the most remote regions of the southwestern United States. Still, it remains one of the most-visited tourist sites in North America.

NATURE AT WORK

Millions of years in the past, raindrops fell on the mostly flat surface of the Colorado Plateau. They began to trickle off the rock surface and seek a course to the ocean. The rainwater etched tiny grooves into the surface. Each time it rained the shape and depth of the grooves were enlarged. Gradually the veinlike pattern of a drainage system became visible. Sand, silt, and rock debris carried by the water continued their patient task of cutting deeper and deeper into the plateau. Nature engaged in creating a physical masterpiece. The final result was the Grand Canyon.

◀ *Millions of years of erosion by the Colorado River has resulted in the natural wonder of the Grand Canyon. Here, Deer Creek flows through sandstone cliffs in Grand Canyon National Park.*

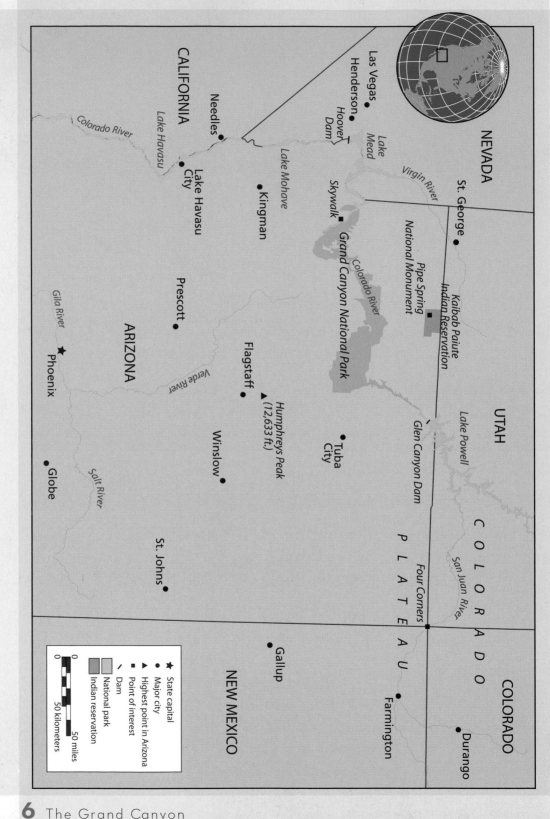

GEOPOLITICAL MAP OF THE GRAND CANYON

NEVADA

CALIFORNIA

Las Vegas
Henderson
Hoover
Dam

Colorado River

Lake
Havasu

Needles

Lake Havasu
City

Lake Mohave

Lake
Mead

Kingman

Skywalk

Grand Canyon National Park

St. George

Virgin River

Pipe Spring
National Monument

Kaibab Paiute
Indian Reservation

Colorado River

UTAH

Lake Powell

Glen Canyon Dam

San Juan River

COLORADO

P L A T E A U

C O L O R A D O

Four Corners

Durango

Prescott

Gila River

Phoenix

ARIZONA

Verde River

Flagstaff

Humphreys Peak
(12,633 ft.)

Winslow

Tuba
City

Globe

Salt River

St. Johns

Gallup

Farmington

NEW MEXICO

State capital
Major city
Highest point in Arizona
Point of interest
Dam
National park
Indian reservation

0   50 miles
0   50 kilometers

The scale and geologic formation of the Grand Canyon attract large numbers of tourists. Almost 2 billion years of geologic history can be viewed in the exposed rock layers of the canyon. Geologists continue to study the complex processes that created this rare landform.

Geology also helps determine which species of plants and animals survive in the canyon's various habitats, or life zones. The great depth of the canyon contains a series of life zones beginning at the bottom and ending along the canyon's rims. Each life zone is characterized by changes in the major types of plant species in it. Although animals move freely between the zones, most species show a preference for a particular zone.

HUMAN ACTIVITY

The Grand Canyon is located in an arid region that does not encourage human settlement. The steep, rugged walls of the canyon helped prevent development. A small number of native peoples inhabited the canyon in the past. Their descendants maintain a small presence in the canyon and along its rims.

Sixteenth-century Spanish explorers were the first Europeans to view the canyon. They judged it to be uninhabitable and never settled there. Some early U.S. citizens described it as valueless and predicted it would remain an uninhabited area. The period of western expansion in America's history changed that view. The undeveloped nature and unmatched beauty of the canyon attracted a new breed of Americans. These rugged individuals, with a love of the natural environment, promoted protecting the canyon for future generations.

Since the twentieth century, tourism developed into the main economic activity associated with the Grand Canyon. Most tourists experience the canyon by standing along one of its rims. A small number hike to the floor of the canyon, thousands fly over the canyon landscape, and some raft through the canyon on the Colorado River.

Inevitably, the environmental impact of millions of tourists is considerable. Concern for plant and animal life in the canyon has long been the focus of environmentalists. Proposals for mineral extraction and similar commercial usages tend to be closely monitored. For example, the mining of uranium in the canyon involves the potential threat from radioactive materials.

Some individuals consider the canyon sacred land. For others it is a majestic gift of nature. Almost everyone considers the canyon the crown jewel of North America's natural treasures.

A Popular Attraction

The National Park Service, which administers Grand Canyon National Park, ranks it the second most popular national park in the United States. The most visited is the Great Smoky Mountain National Park. In 1919, when Grand Canyon National Park was created, 44,173 people visited the park. Approximately 4.5 million tourists now view its inspiring features each year.

Tourism is the major activity at the Grand Canyon. Here, visitors hike Bright Angel Trail below the South Rim.

Tourism is closely monitored by park officials in order to protect the canyon and its visitors.

TWO

A Natural Wonder

The Colorado Plateau, a major U.S. landform region, is located at the Four Corners, the location where the states of Utah, Colorado, New Mexico, and Arizona meet. The plateau covers approximately 130,000 square miles (336,698 square kilometers) of land. This area is almost as large as the state of Montana.

The surface of much of the plateau is flat and located at an average elevation of 5,200 feet (1,585 meters) above sea level. The plateau also contains buttes, mesas, and basins. Some of the plateau's rivers and streams have cut deep canyons into it.

The Colorado Plateau's most majestic canyon is the Grand Canyon. The Grand Canyon has been recognized as one of the Seven Natural Wonders of the World. Visitors to the canyon are often awestruck by its visual beauty. The view of the canyon and of the Colorado River far below leaves many speechless.

◄ *Red sandstone canyons, cliffs, terraces, and buttes form the Grand Canyon, which is located on the Colorado Plateau.*

THE CANYON'S EXTENT

The Grand Canyon includes all of Grand Canyon National Park and parts of the Havasupai and Hualapai Indian reservations, the Kaibab National Forest, and the Little Colorado River Navajo Tribal Park. The canyon crosses northwestern Arizona in a mostly east-to-west direction for 277 miles (446 km). At least six hundred side canyons join the main canyon. The entire canyon covers 1,904 square miles (4,950 sq km) of territory. As of 2010, parts of the canyon were still unexplored.

The Magnificent Seven

Centuries ago historians made lists of the Seven Wonders of the Ancient World. Since then many other lists of seven wonders have appeared. Almost all lists of the seven Natural Wonders of the World include the Grand Canyon. The most widely accepted list recognizes the Grand Canyon, Mount Everest, the Great Barrier Reef, Victoria Falls, the Harbor of Rio de Janeiro, Paricutín Volcano, and the northern lights (aurora borealis).

The Grand Canyon is a major landform that spreads across more than 1,900 square miles (4,920 sq km) and can be as deep as 6,000 feet (1,829 m).

The average width of the canyon is 10 miles (16 km); it is 18 miles (29 km) at its widest point. From the South Rim the canyon plunges approximately a mile (1.6 km) to the Colorado River. At its greatest depth the canyon is 6,000 feet (1,829 m) below the South Rim. The North Rim of the canyon has an average elevation of 8,000 feet (2,400 m). It is approximately 2,000 feet (600 m) higher than the South Rim.

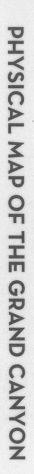

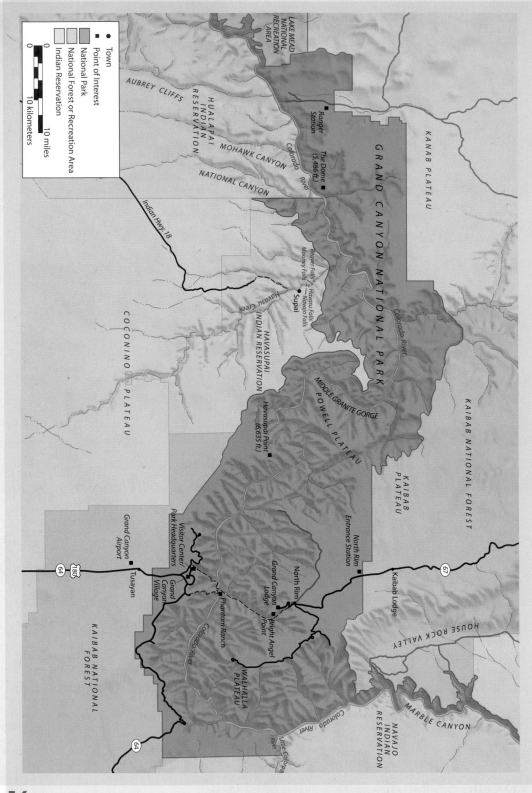

Town
Point of Interest
National Park
National Forest or Recreation Area
Indian Reservation

0
0
10 miles
10 kilometers

LAKE MEAD NATIONAL RECREATION AREA

AUBREY CLIFFS

HUALAPAI INDIAN RESERVATION

MOHAWK CANYON

NATIONAL CANYON

Colorado River

Ranger Station

The Dome (5,486 ft.)

Beaver Falls
Mooney Falls
Havasu Creek
Navajo Falls
Supai

Indian Hwy 18

COCONINO PLATEAU

HAVASUPAI INDIAN RESERVATION

Havasupai Point (6,635 ft.)

MIDDLE GRANITE GORGE

POWELL PLATEAU

GRAND CANYON NATIONAL PARK

KANAB PLATEAU

Colorado River

KAIBAB PLATEAU

KAIBAB NATIONAL FOREST

Grand Canyon Airport

Visitor Center/
Park Headquarters

Grand Canyon Village

Tusayan

64
180

64

KAIBAB NATIONAL FOREST

Phantom Ranch

Colorado River

WALHALLA PLATEAU

Colorado River

Little Colorado River

North Rim Entrance Station

Grand Canyon Lodge
North Rim
Bright Angel Point

Kaibab Lodge

67

HOUSE ROCK VALLEY

NAVAJO INDIAN RESERVATION

MARBLE CANYON

The Mighty Colorado

The Colorado River was the major agent of erosion in the creation of the Grand Canyon. The river begins in Rocky Mountain National Park in Colorado. It flows in a southwesterly direction through western Colorado and southeastern Utah. After entering Arizona, the river passes through Lees Ferry, where the Grand Canyon begins. The river's path then turns westward through the Grand Canyon before flowing into Nevada. The river then turns abruptly and flows due south to the Gulf of California (usually called the Sea of Cortés in Mexico). With a length of 1,450 miles (2,334 km), the Colorado River is the fifth-longest river in the United States.

Here, the Colorado River flows through Marble Canyon. The river is the main agent of erosion that formed the Grand Canyon.

The Colorado River seems out of place as it tumbles through the semiarid-to-arid Grand Canyon. The river carries an impressive amount of water. Much of the water originates in the western Rocky Mountains as snowmelt. Normal flow averages 15,000 cubic feet per second (425 cubic meters per second). Peak flows may reach 50,000 cubic feet per second (1,415 cms). In the canyon the river has an average width of 300 feet (90 m) and an average depth of 40 feet (12 m). The Colorado River has more than one hundred heart-stopping rapids, countless giant boulders, and many dangerous whirlpools.

THE AGE OF ROCKS

To look into the Grand Canyon is to take a peek at the geologic history of the earth itself. The walls of the canyon expose rocks that range in age from 250 million years to almost 2 billion years. All three major

Exotic Streams

When geologists speak of an exotic stream, they do not mean that it is unusual or mysterious. An exotic stream is one that begins in a humid region and ends in an arid region. The Colorado River is one of the world's most striking examples of an exotic stream. Another excellent example is the Nile River, in eastern Africa.

rock types, **igneous**, **metamorphic**, and **sedimentary**, can be found in the canyon. The most common rocks in the canyon are sedimentary and include sandstone, limestone, and shale.

The geologic story of the Grand Canyon's formation begins at the bottom of the canyon. The rocks exposed at the lowest level are known as the Vishnu Basement Rocks. Most of this formation consists of metamorphic and igneous rocks. Then a kind of geologic mystery called an **unconformity** appears. For the next 450 million years any rocks that formed were totally eroded away. Geologists have been unable to explain this mystery.

Immediately above the Vishnu Basement Rocks there are several layers of sedimentary rocks called the Grand Canyon Supergroup. Shale and limestone are the dominant rock types in these layers, but igneous rocks are also found. The supergroup rocks formed between 1.25 billion and 740 million years ago. Any rocks that formed in the next 250 million years have vanished. This period marks the second major unconformity present in the canyon.

The major part of the rock formation process began around 525 million years ago. Beginning then and continuing for the next 300 million years, most of the visible rock layers of the present-day Grand Canyon formed. Large inland seas appeared and disappeared at various times. Sometimes the land was completely underwater, and at other times it was exposed. During at least one period shifting sand dunes covered the area. Fossils found in some of these rock layers provide clues as to what the environment was like at a given

A hiker views ancient rocks of the Inner Gorge in the Grand Canyon. Different types of minerals within the rocks create different colors within the rock walls.

geologic time period. Similar fossils are found in other parts of the world. Their presence helps scientists understand the physical conditions of each region. All of the fossils found in the Grand Canyon predate the dinosaurs.

Over the millennia sandstone, shale, and limestone developed, layer upon layer. Shales, being softer, eroded more easily than the harder limestones and sandstones. The different rates of erosion created the familiar stair-step cliffs of some of the canyon walls. The different types of minerals found in each layer contribute to the array of colors seen in the canyon's rock walls.

The topmost layer of rock is called the Kaibab Limestone. It formed 250 million years ago. Most geologists believe that additional rock layers formed above the Kaibab Limestone, but that erosion caused them to disappear.

CARVING A MASTERPIECE

Some rocks in the Grand Canyon are among the oldest on the North American continent. However, the Grand Canyon is a very young landform in terms of geologic time. For many years geologists estimated that the entire canyon was approximately 6 million years old. A recent study by scientists indicates that the western portion of the canyon is 17 million years old and the eastern is 6 million years old. This study proposes that two major river systems began to carve the canyon as the Colorado Plateau experienced a shift. As the land moved, the rivers cut downward. Eventually, the two rivers joined to form the major course of the Colorado River. Scientists responsible for the study have been unable to determine the date or location that the two rivers joined.

As it carved the Grand Canyon, the Colorado River proved to be an effective agent of erosion. The silt and sand carried by the river increased the ability of the water to cut through the rock layers. The sediment worked like sandpaper to scrape and scour the rock surface on the bottom and along the edges of the river. Seasonal floods enhanced the erosional power of the river. The river carried so much sediment that the color of the water was a murky reddish brown.

The Colorado River deepened the Grand Canyon over the course of several million years. As long as its waters were undammed, the river retained its erosional powers. The construction of the Glen Canyon Dam across the Colorado River in 1963 weakened the

river's erosive force. The dam, which was constructed just above the entrance to the Grand Canyon, was built to store water, to prevent flooding, and to generate electricity. Along with its beneficial contibutions, construction of the dam inevitably caused a certain amount of environmental damage.

The dam blocked sediment that had previously accelerated erosion. The reduction of sediment changed the color of the river's water from reddish brown to greenish blue. The average rate of flow of the river through the canyon also decreased substantially.

CAVES AND WATERFALLS

Roughly a thousand caves dot the canyon. Park officials have recorded the locations of 335 caves. Most are found in the limestone layers of the canyon. The acidity of rain and groundwater can dissolve the minerals in limestone. This process eventually leads to cave formation. Prehistoric animals and native peoples used the caves for shelter.

For safety reasons the National Park Service prohibits tourists from entering the caves. There is one exception; tourists are allowed to visit the Cave of the Domes, on

◁ *Through the power of water, sand, and silt the Colorado River carved the majestic Grand Canyon.*

the Horseshoe Mesa. The Cave of the Domes features many **speleothems**. Speleothems are formations created by the dripping of water within a cave. The water contains a mineral called calcite; as the calcite slowly crystallizes it forms stalactites, stalagmites, and columns. Early visitors to the Cave of the Domes found mummified corpses of ice age animals. Several American-Indian artifacts were discovered in the cave as well.

Majestic waterfalls occur in many parts of the canyon. The total number of waterfalls is unknown. Some waterfalls exist only for a short time during the seasonal snowmelt on the canyon rims. Other waterfalls flow briefly after heavy rains.

It is generally agreed that the most beautiful waterfalls are located on the Havasupai Reservation in the western portion of the canyon. Four major waterfalls discharge aqua-blue water into Havasu Creek before it enters the Colorado River. These waterfalls—Mooney, Havasu, Navajo, and Beaver Falls—are among

The most beautiful waterfalls in the Grand ▸▸ *Canyon are found on the Havasupai Reservation. Havasu Falls is pictured here.*

the main tourist attractions in the canyon. Stunning pools of water at the base of the falls are popular swimming areas for escaping the heat. The water temperature is a fairly consistent 70 degrees Fahrenheit (21.1 degrees Celsius) throughout the year.

Two Different Worlds

The weather and climate on the rims of the canyon are very different from those at the bottom of the canyon. The Bright Angel Ranger Station on the North Rim regularly records the coolest and wettest weather conditions. Phantom Ranch Weather Station at the bottom of the canyon records the hottest and driest conditions. The difference in elevation between these stations—from 5,000 to 6,000 feet (1,525–1,830 m)—is the major cause of the climatic differences. Phantom Ranch recorded the hottest temperature in the canyon: 120 °F (48.9 °C). Bright Angel registered the coldest temperature: −22 °F (−30 °C).

Annual snowfall at the North Rim averages 142 inches (360 centimeters). Most roads along the North Rim close in the winter months because of deep snow. At the South Rim the average is 58 inches (147 cm). On the canyon floor less than an inch (2.5 cm) of snow falls each year, and rain is scarce. In July and August there is a short monsoon season during which most rainfall occurs. Summer storms sometimes produce violent weather conditions with dangerous lightning and flash floods.

Snow covers the canyons and trees of the Grand Canyon as seen from the South Rim.

THREE

Canyon Life

A large variety of plants and animals lives in the Grand Canyon. Multiple **ecosystems** exist within the canyon and along its rims. While little life is found on the canyon's steep rock walls, life is abundant near its springs, rivers, creeks, and waterfalls. Habitats form and change because of temperature, precipitation, soil, slope, exposure to sunlight, and the impact of humans.

Elevation plays a major role in plant and animal life in the Grand Canyon. Specific elevations are associated with distinctive zones of vegetation growth and animal distribution. In the lowest elevations of the canyon, a narrow zone of true desert exists. It extends from the Colorado River to an elevation of 3,500 feet (1,070 m). The next zone, extending from 3,500 feet (1,070 m) to 6,200 feet (1,890 m), is a semiarid zone with patches of grass, scrub brush, pinyon pine, and Utah juniper. The third zone, located between 6,500 feet (1,980 m) and 8,200 feet (2,500 m), is noted for its stunning ponderosa pine forests. The final zone is found above 8,000 feet (2,440 m) and is

◀ *Mountain lions are attracted to the desert zone of the Grand Canyon, where they find a variety of prey.*

Though a desert environment exists at the bottom of the Grand Canyon, shrubs and grasses can be found along the river's edge.

located only along the canyon's North Rim. The dominant vegetation in this zone is a mixed conifer forest; there are also grassland meadows. These zones are not sharply defined and have broad areas of transition from one to the other.

Vegetation zones in the canyon are also related to temperature and precipitation. Less than 10 inches (254 millimeters) of precipitation falls along the canyon's floor; 35 inches (889 mm) fall on the North Rim. It is very hot at the lower elevations and cool to cold at the highest elevations. The species of plants found in each zone are those that have adapted to their environment. Animals move freely among all of the vegetation zones, though many prefer to live in a specific zone.

DESERT ZONE

At the bottom of the canyon is a desert environment. Although temperatures frequently exceed 100 °F (37.8 °C) and rain seldom falls, a ribbon of green runs through the heart of this desert environment. This narrow stretch of green, located in patches along the edge of the Colorado River and its many tributary creeks, supports a **riparian**, or river, ecosystem. Willows, cottonwood trees, dense shrubs, and several nonnative plant species flourish along the riverbanks. After rare summer thunderstorms, wildflowers explode in a variety of colors. There are more plant and animal species along the river than in any other part of the canyon.

Most of the large mammals in the canyon visit or live along the river. The large number of available prey attracts mountain lions, foxes, coyotes, bobcats, and other predators. Beavers cut willows and cottonwood trees for food and to build lodges.

Beavers are found in the river's waters gathering wood for food and as material to build their homes.

At least 250 different bird species have been spotted along the river. Some nest and raise their young in the dense vegetation; others migrate through the canyon on their way to distant locations. Bald eagles feed on the trout in the river.

Insects, a major source of food for birds, are also numerous along the river. Flies, midges, beetles, moths, and butterflies are abundant. Spiders and scorpions are also present.

Reptiles prefer to live in the dense vegetation near the river. Lizards are especially common. One common lizard, the chuckwalla, is the second-largest lizard in the United States. To escape a predator, the chuckwalla will crawl deep into a crevasse in the rocks and

The Scorpion's Sting

One of the most common creatures along the river corridor is the scorpion. The giant hairy scorpion (left) and the bark scorpion are the best-known species. The giant hairy scorpion is the largest scorpion in the United States. Both scorpions have eight legs and a tail with a stinger. Scorpions stab their prey with the stinger and inject venom. The sting is rarely deadly but can be very painful. The bark scorpion has the most toxic venom. Scorpions are nocturnal—that is, they come out at night.

Lizards are some of the most common animals found deep in the canyon. This is a chuckwalla lizard.

inflate its body. This survival tactic prevents a predator from pulling it out of its hiding place.

The large numbers of lizards and rodents in the river vegetation attract snakes. There are more than twenty different species of snakes in the canyon. Six of these species are rattlesnakes, including the Grand Canyon pink rattlesnake. Rattlesnakes possess fangs that inject toxic venom into their victims. Fortunately, they are timid by nature and will strike at humans only if they feel threatened.

A short distance from the river's edge, the ribbon of life disappears, and the surface turns grey and brown. Plants are scarce here, and animals struggle to stay alive in a zone where water is difficult to find. The soil is thin and holds little moisture.

The Grand Canyon pink rattlesnake is one of six species of rattlesnakes found in the canyon.

The daytime heat can be unbearable. Place-names such as Furnace Flats, Hell's Hollow, and Cremation Canyon reflect the harsh conditions. To survive, plants must adapt special ways to conserve water.

Plants that can live in environments with limited water are called **xerophytes**. Some xerophytes have a long taproot that enables them to reach water far below the surface. Other plants have broad root systems that capture rainwater after a short downpour. Most xerophytes have small leaves that are covered with hair or with a waxy coating; these coverings help the plant limit its water loss. Almost all xerophytes have cells capable of storing water. Thorns are also common on these plants; the thorns prevent animals from nibbling on their leaves.

A variety of cacti is common in the desert zone. The barrel cactus and the prickly pear cactus are common throughout the canyon. American Indians living in the canyon scraped the thorns off new prickly pear

Prickly pear cactus thrive in the ▶▶
Grand Canyon.

FOUR

Echoes of the Past

A visitor viewing the Grand Canyon from either the North Rim or the South Rim experiences a sense of wonder. Time seems to stand still as the viewer tries to imagine how long it took for the canyon's rock walls to form. The rock layers below the viewer's feet reveal almost 2 billion years of the earth's history. The canyon itself is a mere 6 to 17 million years old. Human presence in the canyon is little more than the blink of an eye in geologic time.

Between 10,000 and 11,000 years ago the first humans arrived in the Grand Canyon. Known as the Paleoindians, they were migratory hunters and gatherers who did not establish permanent settlements. The Archaic culture followed the Paleoindians. These early native peoples established temporary camps approximately four thousand years ago. By 500 CE the Anasazi, the ancestors of present-day Pueblo Indians, had developed permanent settlements in the canyon and on its rims. By the late 1200s they had abandoned most of their settlements. About 1300 the ancestors of today's Havasupai and Hualapai tribes arrived along the canyon's West Rim and river corridor. The Paiute and Navajo Indian tribes followed at a later date.

◄ *The Havasupai settled in the Grand Canyon almost seven hundred years ago.*

The Conquistadors

In 1521 the Spanish conquest of the Aztecs in what is now Mexico City established Spain's control over a large area. Spanish land claims reached across most of the American Southwest and included the Grand Canyon. Although most of the area was unexplored, the Spanish crown claimed it as a part of its domain.

The Spanish **conquistadors** (their word for "conquerors") were unaware of the existence of the Grand Canyon. A party of explorers, led by García López de Cárdenas, discovered it in 1540 while searching

García López de Cárdenas is led by an American-Indian guide to the edge of the Grand Canyon.

Francisco Vásquez de Coronado

Francisco Vásquez de Coronado (c. 1510–1554) arrived in Mexico (New Spain) in 1535. Within three years he was appointed governor of Nueva Galicia, a region on the western side of the new Spanish empire. His reputation as a competent and fair administrator led to his appointment to command an expedition to search for the Seven Cities of Cíbola, believed to contain vast treasures. The expedition was also expected to conquer the region and claim it as Spanish territory. Coronado spent two and a half years searching for riches without success. His failure to find gold and silver disappointed the Spanish officials in Mexico City. They removed him from his post as governor of Nueva Galicia in 1544, and he retired to a quiet life in Mexico City.

for the fabled Seven Cities of Cíbola, which were rumored to hold vast treasures of gold and silver. Francisco Vásquez de Coronado was in charge of the expedition. However, it was Cárdenas's party that was led to the rim of the canyon by Hopi Indian guides.

During the expedition Coronado was told of a great river that crossed the region. Rivers are always of interest to explorers because they are associated with farming areas, transportation routes, and supplies of freshwater. Coronado divided his large expeditionary force into several parts. He chose García López de Cárdenas, one of his best soldiers, to find out if this great river truly existed.

The size and depth of the canyon overwhelmed Cárdenas and the other Spaniards. At first, they thought the river below was only 6 feet (1.8 m) wide. In reality, the river was more than 300 feet (90 m) wide. Boulders on the side of the canyon that were 200 feet (60 m) to 300 feet (90 m) in height were judged to be the size of a man.

After three days of searching for a path to reach the river, three men began their descent. The three hiked down the dangerous

The Spaniards had a difficult time realizing the sheer immensity of the Grand Canyon from their view on the rim.

slopes all day. Although ultimately unsuccessful in their attempt to reach the river, they were able to confirm that the American Indians had told the truth about the width of the river. They also could see that many of the boulders "were taller than the great tower of Seville" in Spain. The explorers gave up on their attempt to reach the floor of the canyon because of a lack of water. Cárdenas filed a written report of his experience for Coronado. In his report he expressed his disappointment at not discovering riches. He judged the region to hold little value. As a result the Spanish showed little interest in the remarkable feature Cárdenas had described.

Naming a River

In 1776, almost 250 years after Cárdenas's discovery of the canyon, Francisco Tomás Garcés, a Spanish missionary priest, visited the Havasupai Indians in the Grand Canyon. He had traveled alone over 300 miles (480 km) in an attempt to convert the Indians to Christianity. During his visit he observed the reddish-brown-colored waters of the canyon's river and named the river Colorado, from a Spanish word meaning "reddish" or "rose colored." The gorge did not overly impress him; he referred to it as a "prison of cliffs and canyons."

The Spanish largely ignored the Grand Canyon during their nearly three-hundred-year claim (1540–1821) to the region for a number of reasons. The location of the canyon was on the northern edge of their empire. Spanish administrative headquarters in Mexico City were about a thousand miles from the canyon. There were no large Indian populations to convert to Christianity. The area seemed devoid of gold and silver. Travel to the region was difficult and water was scarce. The lack of Spanish interest in this area resulted in little development. The Spanish failed to establish significant military posts, major missions, or agricultural settlements.

THE MEXICAN WAR

In 1821 the Republic of Mexico won its independence from Spain after a lengthy war. The Mexican victory over Spain ended Spanish control of the Southwest. Mexico now had administrative control over the Grand Canyon. They administered the area from head-quarters in Albuquerque, New Mexico. They kept a wary eye on the growing interest in the Southwest held by their powerful northern neighbor, the United States.

Mexico's control over the Grand Canyon lasted less than thirty years. Anger over the American annexation of Texas (Texas had won its own war of independence from Mexico in 1836) led to the Mexican War (1846–1848). This war ended with the signing of the Treaty of Guadalupe Hidalgo on February 2, 1848. In the treaty Mexico surrendered almost half its total territory, including the Grand Canyon, to the United States.

WESTERN EXPANSION

Many Americans were excited about the new land they had gained in the West. The discovery of large gold deposits in California in 1848 helped fuel that excitement. The American public wanted to know more about the potential of their new territory. The federal government ordered new surveys and studies of the region.

One of the first studies commissioned by the U.S. Army was the Ives Expedition (1857–1858). In 1857 Lieutenant Joseph Christmas

Ives was instructed to determine how far boats could travel on the Colorado River. The U.S. Army planned to use the river as a supply route to several military outposts in the region. The military shipped a 54-foot (17-m) steel steamboat, in pieces, to the mouth of the Colorado River on the Gulf of California. The steamboat was then reassembled and began its journey upstream. Before the boat reached the Grand Canyon, it struck a rock just below the site of the present-day Hoover Dam. The disabled boat could go no farther.

Lieutenant Ives and his team left the boat and walked along the rim of the canyon. At Diamond Creek they hiked to the floor of the canyon before ending the expedition. When Ives returned from his journey he made the following statement: "The region last explored is, of course, altogether valueless. It can be approached only from the south, and after entering it there is nothing to do but to leave. Ours has been the first, and will doubtless be the last, party of whites to visit this profitless locality. It seems intended by nature that the Colorado River, along the greater portion of its lonely and majestic way, shall be forever unvisited and undisturbed." Apparently Ives was unaware that white fur trappers and Spanish conquistadors had visited the canyon earlier.

Not every member of the Ives Expedition shared Ives's opinion. The expedition's scientist, John Strong Newberry, was impressed with the geology of the canyon. He encouraged his friend and fellow geologist, Major John Wesley Powell, to visit and study the Grand Canyon.

An American Hero

On May 24, 1869, Major John Wesley Powell and nine other men began an epic adventure. They planned to follow the Green River from Wyoming to the Colorado River. Once on the Colorado River, they would float on the river's water through the unexplored depths of the Grand Canyon. The plan was to use four wooden boats during a three-month, thousand-mile (1,600-km) trip through uncharted wilderness. There were no completely reliable maps to guide their way. For this reason alone many observers considered their goal foolish. They predicted that once the men entered the canyon, they would never be seen or heard from again.

Powell did not share these concerns. He was a battle-tested Civil War veteran who had lost an arm at Shiloh. To him and his nine companions, the canyon and the Colorado River were simply two new challenges. Early in the trip they lost a boat and one-third of their supplies and equipment. Even when one member of the team left, the rest pushed onward. The river's violent rapids and whirlpools seriously damaged their boats. They made use of driftwood to repair the boats and to carve new oars. They themselves were almost as badly beaten as the boats by the turbulent waters. When their food supply dwindled they ate apples and moldy flour.

On August 27, 1869, three more members of the group decided to leave the expedition. They walked out of the canyon on August 28 and were killed mysteriously a few days later. Powell and the remaining

Major John Wesley Powell's expedition ran the rapids of the Grand Canyon.

five team members completed the journey two days later. Powell's report of the journey generated national interest in the Grand Canyon. The modern fascination with this natural wonder had begun.

STRIKING IT RICH

After the discovery of gold at Sutter's Mill in north-central California in 1848, prospectors began to arrive at the Grand Canyon. They panned some fine gold dust from creeks that had built up deposits near the Colorado River. They built trails along the rock walls and dug holes and mine shafts throughout the canyon. A few locations yielded some gold, silver, copper, and asbestos. Most mine claims proved to be worthless. The canyon was not a good location to engage in mining. Its remoteness made moving supplies to potential mines both difficult and expensive. Transporting ore out of the canyon was also difficult and costly. Abandoned mine sites can still be seen scattered throughout the canyon.

CHANGING ATTITUDES

The last half of the nineteenth century was a period of widespread development in the American West. Railroads crossed the continent and opened up new opportunities. Settlers established large ranches, harvested timber, and mined the earth. Protection of the environment was largely ignored.

Gradually attitudes toward preservation and development began to change. People interested in protecting the country's national

Captain John Hance

In 1883 Captain John Hance became the first white man to establish a permanent settlement on the canyon rim. He personally built the Hance Trail to the canyon floor. He mined asbestos for a few years, but soon discovered that he could make more money guiding tourists on treks into the canyon. Hance captured his clients' attention with his skills as a master storyteller. He could spin yarns around the campfire for hours. In his later years Hance worked as a greeter at one of the canyon's facilities; guests enjoyed his many humorous anecdotes and tall tales. One of Hance's best-known stories deals with the formation of the Grand Canyon.

It was hard work and took a long time but I dug it myself, with a pick and a shovel and a wheelbarrow, and if you want to know what I done with the dirt, just go out east here and look south through a clearin' through the trees and you will see it, stacked up about 50 miles away. I wheeled it over there in my wheelbarrow and stacked it up nearly 13,000 feet high so as it wouldn't clutter things up here on the canyon rim; and you might not believe it, but they call that pile of dirt and rocks the San Francisco Peaks nowadays.

—from the Museum Collection
of Grand Canyon National Park

treasures raised their voices. Many of them wanted the Grand Canyon to be designated a protected area. Senator Benjamin Harrison of Indiana submitted bills to the Senate in 1882, 1883, and 1886 that would have created Grand Canyon National Park. Each bill was defeated.

In 1888 Harrison was elected president. In 1893, with an executive order, he created the Grand Canyon Forest Reserve. This action limited development in the canyon. Later, in 1906, President Theodore Roosevelt established the Grand Canyon Game Preserve. On February 26, 1919, with President Woodrow Wilson's signing of the Grand Canyon National Park Act, the National Park Service took over the administration and protection of America's newest national park.

CHANGES FOR VISITORS

Most early visitors to the Grand Canyon arrived by stagecoach. It was a long, hard, and dusty trip. In 1901 the Atchison, Topeka, and Santa Fe Railroad extended a rail line from Williams, Arizona, to the canyon's rim. Soon thousands of tourists arrived to gaze at the physical beauty of nature's masterpiece. As highways improved, automobiles gradually replaced the train as the major means of transportation to the canyon.

The Grand Canyon was once a difficult place to explore. Modern technology has helped subdue some of its perils so that visitors can safely experience this natural wonder firsthand. John Wesley

HARPER'S
WEEKLY

EDITED BY GEORGE HARVEY

Powell and his crew risked their lives boating down the mighty Colorado River. While many dangerous rapids are still present, modern rafting equipment reduces substantially the risk of serious injury or death. Food, water, and shelter are more available than in the past. Helicopters and mules are available to carry tourists from the rim to the canyon floor. New global positioning system technology helps hikers find their way in the canyon and can prevent explorers from getting lost.

A 1911 edition of Harper's Weekly featured tourism to the Grand Canyon on its cover.

FIVE

Living in Harmony

There have been human beings present in the Grand Canyon area for at least ten thousand years. Several cultures, including the Paleoindians, Archaic peoples, Anasazi, Kaibab Paiute, Hualapai, Havasupai, Navajo, and Hopi peoples, have left their imprint. The Spanish, who arrived in the sixteenth century, paid little attention to the region when it was part of their empire.

PALEOINDIANS, ARCHAIC PEOPLES, AND ANASAZI

Archaeologists believe the first human presence in the Grand Canyon occurred between 10,000 and 11,000 years ago. The earliest people are known as the Paleoindian culture. Although little is known about their culture, most scientists believe Paleoindians were highly mobile hunters. They hunted prehistoric mammals such as mammoths, ground sloths, camels, and mountain goats. These early

◄ American Indians have called the Grand Canyon home for thousands of years. Here a Navajo girl tends her sheep on the Navajo Indian Reservation in the Grand Canyon.

peoples did not establish permanent settlements but lived in small camps and moved frequently. The Paleoindians were in the Grand Canyon area for three thousand years.

The Archaic peoples, whose civilization was formerly called the Desert Culture, followed the Paleoindian culture. These peoples occupied the Colorado Plateau for four thousand to six thousand years. Evidence suggests they arrived in the Grand Canyon four thousand years ago (roughly 2000 BCE). They lived in caves and under rock shelves for protection from the weather. They hunted deer, rabbits, squirrels, birds, and other game. Seeds and berries were also an important part of their diet.

The Archaic peoples left artistic evidence of their culture: wooden figurines and painted rock art. The most famous rock art site in the canyon is the Shaman's Gallery. The paintings are displayed along a 60-foot-long (18-m-long) wall under a sandstone rock ledge. Images of human-shaped figures as well as bighorn sheep and geometric shapes cover most of the wall. Scientists believe the paintings are at least three thousand years old.

The Anasazi were the ancestors of many of the present-day Pueblo Indian tribes who live in or near the canyon. The Anasazi followed the Archaic peoples and established many sites in the canyon and on both the North and the South rims. The earliest Anasazi appear to have arrived in the canyon sometime after 500 CE. Evidence of their presence in the region suggests they abandoned the area around 1200.

Split-Twig Animals

Small animal figurines made by the Archaic peoples provide some of the earliest evidence of human occupation in the Grand Canyon. The animal figures are called split-twig figurines because each one is made from a single, small branch of willow tree. The twig was first split with a sharp stone tool from its top to near its base. The artisan then twisted and wrapped the two halves into the shape of a deer or bighorn sheep. The size of the miniature animals ranged from 2 to 7.5 inches (50–190 mm). Sometimes an animal figure was pierced by a single twig to represent a kill made while hunting or to ensure good luck hunting.

During their occupation of the area, many of the characteristics of their material culture began to change. The Anasazi became more settled and built small villages of stone houses. The development of ceramic pottery blossomed. Artisans used fibers from agave and yucca to weave baskets with beautiful designs. The Anasazi also began to farm and grow crops such as maize (corn), squash, and beans. Primitive irrigation systems carried water to the fields. Granaries were cut into the walls of the canyon 500 feet (152 m) above the Colorado River. These granaries were most likely used to store seed grains.

Ancient Indian rock art is seen at Shamon's Gallery in the canyon.

Anasazi ruins can be seen in the cliffs above the Colorado River.

Shortly after 1250 the Anasazi began to abandon their canyon homes and farm plots. Many scientists believe that they left because of a severe and lengthy drought. As of 2010 there were more than two thousand known Anasazi archaeological sites within Grand Canyon National Park.

THE KAIBAB PAIUTE

The Grand Canyon appears to have been largely uninhabited by humans for the next century. Gradually, ancestors of the American Indians that now occupy the region settled near or in the canyon.

land along the Colorado River. Dramatic scenery, including mesas, buttes, vertical cliffs, and pine forests, attract increasing numbers of tourists annually to the reservation.

Tourism is now the major source of income for the Hualapai. Anyone entering the reservation must pay a fee. They own and operate the only American-Indian river rafting company on the Colorado River. Diamond Creek Road is the only road that leads to the bottom of the Grand Canyon. Tourists must purchase permits to drive on the road. The Hualapai also sell big-game hunting permits and serve as guides for hunters. The latest Hualapai tourist attraction is the Skywalk, which opened in 2007.

Local dancers of the Hualapai Nation perform for tourists at the Skywalk.

The Hualapai believe the Skywalk will bring major new income to the reservation. With few other economic activities to support the population, money generated from tourism is important to help lift the Hualapai out of poverty. While Grand Canyon National Park attracts approximately 4.5 million people each year, the Hualapai Reservation receives only 250,000 tourists annually. If tourist numbers grow as expected, jobs will be created, wages will increase, and the standard of living for the Hualapai will improve.

The Skywalk

The Skywalk is a steel and glass footbridge that extends 70 feet (21 m) out over the canyon. The horseshoe-shaped platform can support 70 tons (64 metric tons) of weight. Tourists standing on the Skywalk are surrounded by 4-inch-thick (102-mm-thick) walls of protective glass as they look into the canyon 4,000 feet (1,220 m) below.

THE HAVASUPAI

The Havasupai Indians moved into the Grand Canyon region approximately seven hundred years ago. They established the oldest permanent settlement within the canyon along Havasu Creek. This land is sacred to the Havasupai. It is their belief that their creator, Tudjupa, gave them the land.

The Havasupai lived in brush and mud huts called **wickiups** and cultivated maize, beans, and squash in the summers. During the winters they moved onto the canyon's rim, where they hunted wild game and gathered edible wild plants. This cycle continued for centuries. In 1882 the federal government restricted the Havasupai to a 518-acre (209-ha) reservation in Havasu Canyon. In 1975 the reservation was expanded to 188,077 acres (76,112 ha), which included part of the plateau above the canyon.

Most of the Havasupai still living on the reservation live deep in the canyon in and around the village of Supai. This small settlement has a school, a small grocery store, tribal offices, a post office, and little else. The pride of the Havasupai people in their culture can be seen in the fact that all of them still use their own language.

Tourism is the major source of income for the Havasupai. Despite the absence of roads, approximately 12,000 visitors come to the reservation each year. The tourists hike or ride mules or horses from the canyon rim. A few tourists arrive by helicopter. Major attractions are four beautiful waterfalls with blue-green waters. Their tribal council

Most Havasupai reside in this village deep in the Grand Canyon.

strictly limits the number of visitors each year. In addition, visitors are not allowed to bring alcohol, guns, or pets on the reservation, nor can they light campfires.

The Mule Express

The branch of the U.S. Postal Service in Supai is the only one in the country where the vehicles used to deliver mail are mules. All postcards mailed from the Supai post office are stamped with a special postmark: "Mule Train Mail—Havasupai Indian Reservation."

THE NAVAJO

Numbering about 300,000, the Navajo are the second-largest group of American Indians in the United States. About 60 percent live on the Navajo Indian Reservation, the largest reservation in the United States. Navajo land includes more than 16 million acres (6.5 ha). Some of this land borders the eastern part of the South Rim of the Grand Canyon.

The Navajo migrated to the Grand Canyon from western Canada. During their early occupation they were nomadic hunters and gatherers. By the early eighteenth century they began to form small agricultural settlements. They raised large numbers of sheep and cultivated corn. They built permanent houses called hogans, which had six or eight sides and a single door facing the rising sun. Herding was the Navajo's major economic activity by the early nineteenth century. Herds of sheep numbered in the hundreds of thousands. The Navajo became famous for their hand-woven woolen blankets.

SIX

Concerns for the Future

Most Americans cherish the Grand Canyon as a national treasure. There is a strong national interest in protecting this resource. Some individuals, however, believe that the nation has not been a good protector of the canyon and that poor decisions have been made in the management of its plant and animal life. They point out that human decisions have resulted in the extinction of important native plant and animal species and express concern for species that are now endangered. Mining issues, particularly those dealing with uranium, also have been and continue to be controversial topics.

A HUNK OF CONCRETE

The construction of Glen Canyon Dam 15 miles (26 km) above the entrance of the Grand Canyon was completed in 1963. Although many supported the building of the dam, some now believe it has been a disaster for the canyon and want it removed.

◀ *The Grand Canyon is viewed as one of the world's most treasured natural wonders.*

The dam was built to provide water storage in an arid region. Because of water's scarcity, its release is controlled. Los Angeles, Phoenix, Tucson, Las Vegas, and other large cities get some of the water. Farms in Arizona, California, Nevada, and Mexico also get water from the dam. The dam's large hydroelectric generators that produce electricity that is distributed over a broad region. In addition, Lake Powell catches sediment from the Colorado River that would clog Lake Mead, behind the Hoover Dam.

Inevitably, the building of the dam caused Glen Canyon to be flooded. The dam eliminates the annual floods that were an important aspect of the Grand Canyon's physical environment. Beaches and sandbars that provided habitats for certain plants

The Glen Canyon Dam is viewed by some ▶▶
as harmful to the natural environment of the Grand Canyon. It was built for flood control, water storage, and electrical generation.

and animals disappeared. The lack of sand and silt also slowed the natural rate of erosion in the canyon.

The water discharged from the dam is cold all year round. The constant cold water has led to the extinction of some native fish species; others have been endangered. The colder water temperature also increases the risk of hypothermia for swimmers and rafters.

Opponents of the dam argue that it wastes water. Statistics released by the Bureau of Reclamation show that more water enters Lake Powell than leaves it. The annual loss of water due to evaporation and seepage is estimated at nearly a million acre-feet. One opponent of the construction of the Glen Canyon Dam called it "America's most regretted environmental mistake."

Glen Canyon Dam

Construction of the Glen Canyon Dam began in 1959. The dam's height, 710 feet (216 m) above the floor of the canyon, makes it the second-highest dam in the United States. Its width is 1,560 feet (475 m). Lake Powell, the reservoir created by the dam, covers 266 square miles (689 sq km) when full. It took seventeen years for the reservoir to fill completely. The shoreline of the lake extends for 1,960 miles (3,150 km).

UNWANTED GUESTS

Several species of plants and animals that are not native to the Grand Canyon now live among the native plants and animals. Some were introduced to the canyon intentionally. Other species arrived accidentally or by unknown processes. These species are referred to as exotic, nonnative, or introduced species. Frequently these nonnative species have a negative impact on the native species.

Examples of nonnative species of plants that have invaded large areas are tamarisk, camelthorn, Sahara mustard, and cheatgrass. In some locations these plants have crowded out the major native species and seriously altered the ecosystem.

Tamarisk and camelthorn are plants that are native to both North Africa and the Middle East. Large stands of these plants are now found along the Colorado River corridor, where they are replacing the native cottonwoods and willow groves. Tamarisk (salt cedar) is a plant whose roots can grow to depths of 100 feet (30 m). The long roots enable the plant to suck the soil moisture from native plants; without moisture the plants die. In addition, the leaves of the tamarisk contain high amounts of salt; as the leaves fall from the plant and decay, the soil becomes salty. A high salt content in the soil can stunt the growth of native plants or kill them.

Camelthorn is an equally destructive plant. Its broad root system is able to reach water 50 feet (15 m) below the surface and also to spread 26 feet (8 m) from the main trunk. Native plants in the same area frequently die from a lack of available water. Both tamarisk and camelthorn create a habitat less welcoming to mammals, birds, rodents, reptiles, and insects than do cottonwoods and willows. Once established, both plants are almost impossible to destroy.

Sahara mustard is one of the newest nonnative plants that pose a threat to the Grand Canyon ecosystems. It spreads rapidly, and its broad leaves smother native plants by blocking out sunshine. The plant's broad root system also robs the soil moisture from slower-growing native plants. The Grand Canyon National Park's Science and Resource Management Division developed a program to halt the spread of Sahara mustard. The division recruited volunteers from the local community, several U.S. states, and South Korea. The volunteers succeeded in removing many of the invasive plants before they could spread over larger areas and choke out the native plants.

Cheatgrass has had a very destructive impact on the native grasses of the pinyon pine and Utah juniper scrub forest and grassland zone. Cheatgrass dies in midsummer after producing thousands of seeds. The seeds **germinate** in the fall and grow rapidly during the winter. The grass quickly establishes a large root system and steals most of the water from the soil before native grasses begin their spring growth. Native grasses decline, and the cheatgrass and other invasive plants take over. Many grazing animals seem to dislike the taste of cheatgrass. Avoidance of the cheatgrass in favor of the shrinking supply of native grasses leads to overgrazing.

Rainbow trout and brown trout are two species of nonnative fish that were introduced into the Colorado River below the Glen Canyon

Dam in the 1960s. Prior to the construction of the dam, trout could not survive in the river as it flowed through the canyon in the summer, when water temperatures reached 80 °F (27 °C). Trout are a cold-water species and require much lower water temperatures. The water that is released from the Glen Canyon Dam is a fairly consistent 47 °F (8.3 °C), a perfect temperature for trout. Trout are now the major species of fish in the river.

Prospectors first introduced burros, or donkeys, into the Grand Canyon in the nineteenth century. The tourist industry later used them as pack animals to accompany hikers to lower canyon

A burro peeks out over the Grand Canyon terrain.

campgrounds. Over time some of the burros were intentionally released into the wild. Other burros wandered away from camps and became feral (wild). Over the years a large herd of feral burros spread out through the canyon.

The feral burros competed with native grazing species, such as desert bighorn sheep, for scarce grasses. In areas where their numbers were especially high, the burros overgrazed the native plants. Overgrazing led to an invasion of nonnative plants as well as soil erosion. The burros tended to gather at springs and creeks to drink. They trampled the vegetation around the water sites and fouled the water with their waste. In the 1920s the National Park Service classified the feral burros as pests and began to eliminate them. Between 1924 and 1931 rangers killed an estimated 1,467 feral burros in the Grand Canyon.

A small number of the feral burros survived in remote areas of the canyon, and the herd began to increase in size again. By the 1970s the burros once again needed to be eliminated. In 1979 the National Park Service reached a conciliatory solution with the Fund for Animals. The Fund for Animals hired experts to capture the feral burros alive and airlift them out of the canyon. Park rangers killed the few that remained during the winter of 1981/1982.

WARNING SIGNS

The complete disappearance of an individual plant or animal species from a region causes major concern among environmentalists.

These losses may be warning signs that the health of an ecosystem is in danger. Some examples of species that no longer exist in the Grand Canyon are grizzly bears, black-footed ferrets, otters, and gray wolves. Most scientists believe that the major cause of their disappearance was hunting or habitat destruction.

In the Grand Canyon section of the Colorado River, four native fish species can no longer be found: the Colorado pikeminnow, razorback sucker, bonytail chub, and roundtail chub. Lower water temperatures resulting from the construction of the Glen Canyon Dam is the major reason for the loss of these species. Nonnative predator fish, such as trout, also contributed to the problem.

The northern leopard frog has not been observed in the canyon for years. The loss of this species of amphibian is a reflection of a broader world problem of declining amphibian populations. Amphibians are considered to be indicator species—that is, their decline is a sign that the environmental health of the earth is also declining. Factors that may be contributing to the decline are climate change, toxic chemicals, nonnative predators, habitat destruction, and new diseases.

The northern leopard frog has not been seen in the Grand Canyon for some time, a sure sign of environmental issues within the canyon.

A Rare Bird

In the early 1980s, the California condor was no longer present in the Grand Canyon and was on the brink of extinction. The condor was reintroduced into the canyon in 1996 as a result of a captive breeding program. As of 2010 approximately sixty of these magnificent birds were thriving above the rims of the canyon.

The largest land bird in North America, a mature condor can weigh more than 20 pounds (9 kilograms) and have a wingspan of almost 10 feet (3 m). Condors are scavengers that eat only the meat of dead animals. When they search for food, they use thermal updrafts to soar at speeds up to 50 miles (80 km) per hour. They may travel up to 100 miles (160 km) in a single day searching for a meal.

ENDANGERED SPECIES

The placement of an animal or plant species on the endangered species list raises environmental concerns. Some species of particular concern in the Grand Canyon are the humpback chub, the Kanab ambersnail, and the southwestern willow flycatcher. Sentry milk vetch is the only plant in the canyon that has been placed on the endangered species list.

The decline of the humpback chub is of special interest to scientists. They believe it has inhabited the Colorado River for at least 2 million years. Hundreds of thousands of these small fish used to be present in the river as it flowed through the Grand Canyon. By 2000 their numbers had been reduced to roughly a thousand. The humpback chub requires warm, murky water for spawning. The much lower water temperatures in the river that resulted from the building of the Glen Canyon Dam caused a significant decline in the species. Nonnative trout, which not only competed for food with the humpback chub but also ate the chub, contributed to their decline.

The Kanab ambersnail is on the verge of extinction. There are only two known natural populations in the Southwest. One is located in private wetlands in southern Utah; the other is at Vasey's Paradise, a large spring and waterfall in the eastern end of the Grand Canyon. Less than two thousand of these extremely rare snails live in the canyon in low, thick vegetation close to the water.

The southwestern willow flycatcher is an endangered bird. There may be only a thousand breeding pairs of this bird still in existence.

The Grand Canyon is a place of majestic beauty for all to enjoy. Through environmental awareness and protection, the canyon will remain a natural wonder for centuries to come.

WORDS OF WISDOM

In 1903 President Theodore Roosevelt delivered a speech in which he suggested how the Grand Canyon should be treated: "Leave it as it is. You cannot improve on it. The ages have been at work on it, and man can only mar it. What you can do is to keep it for your children, your children's children, and for all who come after you, as one of the great sights which every American if he can travel at all should see."

It seems hard to quarrel with Roosevelt's advice. Both national policy and popular sentiment favor the preservation of the Grand Canyon for future generations to marvel at and enjoy.

ABOUT THE AUTHORS

Byron Augustin is a nationally known Regents' Professor of Geography at Texas State University. His love for geography has given him a passion for traveling. He has visited forty-nine of the fifty U.S. states, twenty-six of Mexico's thirty-one states, eight Canadian provinces, and fifty-five countries on five of the seven continents.

Augustin is the author of twelve books, two book chapters, and twenty-six articles in refereed scholarly journals. Most recently he authored *Andorra* in the Cultures of the World series and *Yellowstone National Park* in the Nature's Wonders series for Marshall Cavendish. He is also a professional photographer. More than 1,100 of his photos have been published worldwide. They have been featured by the National Geographic Society and in *Encyclopedia Britannica*, *Outdoor Life*, and scores of books and magazines.

Jake Kubena teaches geography, Spanish, and martial arts at Katherine Anne Porter School in Wimberley, Texas. He has a bachelor of science degree and a masters of applied geography degree from Texas State University. He has coauthored two books and edited eight geography books. Kubena enjoys traveling. He has been visiting Mexico regularly since childhood. He also has traveled extensively in the United States and Europe.